# Do You Like Taking Care of Animals?

Diane Lindsey Reeves

T0102559

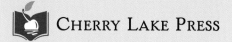
# CHERRY LAKE PRESS

Published in the United States of America by Cherry Lake Publishing Group
Ann Arbor, Michigan
www.cherrylakepublishing.com

Reading Adviser: Beth Walker Gambro, MS, Ed., Reading Consultant, Yorkville, IL

Photo Credits: cover: © skvalval/Shutterstock; page 5: © hedgehog94/Shutterstock (detail); page 6: © Gelpi/ Shutterstock; page 7: © Bildagentur Zoonar GmbH/Shutterstock; page 8: © Monkey Business Images/Shutterstock; page 9: Air Force Staff Sgt. Deven Schultz/U.S. Department of Defense; page 10: © cynoclub/Shutterstock; page 11: © kyslynskahal/Shutterstock; page 12: NPS Photo; page 13: Briana Carmona/NPS Photo; page 14: © Jim Parkin/ Shutterstock; page 15: © Pixel-Shot/Shutterstock; page 16: © Jayme Burrows/Shutterstock; page 17: © demibombe/ Shutterstock; page 18: NOAA; page 19: Kevin Lino NOAA/NMFS/PIFSC/ESD; page 20: © hedgehog94/Shutterstock; page 21: © SritanaN/Shutterstock; page 22: © pritsana/Shutterstock; page 23: © Kzenon/Shutterstock; page 24: © AJR_photo/Shutterstock; page 25: © SeventyFour/Shutterstock; page 26: © topimages/Shutterstock; page 27: © Evannovostro/Shutterstock; page 30: © Krakenimages.com/Shutterstock; page 31: © Elena Sherengovskaya/ Shutterstock

Copyright © 2023 by Cherry Lake Publishing Group

All rights reserved. No part of this book may be reproduced or utilized in any form or by any means without written permission from the publisher.

**Cherry Lake Press** is an imprint of Cherry Lake Publishing Group.

Library of Congress Cataloging-in-Publication Data

Names: Reeves, Diane Lindsey, 1959- author.
Title: Do you like taking care of animals? / written by Diane Lindsey Reeves.
Description: Ann Arbor, Michigan : Cherry Lake Publishing, [2023] | Series: Career clues for kids | Audience: Grades 4-6
Summary: "Do you love animals? That might be a potential clue to your future career! This book explores what a career working with animals might look like. Readers will discover how their interests can lead to a lifelong future career. Aligned to curriculum standards and 21st Century Skills, Career Clues for Kids prepares readers for a successful future. Includes table of contents, glossary, index, sidebars, and author biographies"— Provided by publisher.
Identifiers: LCCN 2022039263 | ISBN 9781668919507 (hardcover) | ISBN 9781668920527 (paperback) | ISBN 9781668923184 (pdf) | ISBN 9781668921852 (ebook)
Subjects: LCSH: Animal specialists—Vocational guidance—Juvenile literature.
Classification: LCC SF80 .R44 2023 | DDC 636.0023—dc23/eng/20220906
LC record available at https://lccn.loc.gov/2022039263

Cherry Lake Publishing Group would like to acknowledge the work of the Partnership for 21st Century Learning, a Network of Battelle for Kids. Please visit *http://www.battelleforkids.org/networks/p21* for more information.

Printed in the United States of America
Corporate Graphics

**Diane Lindsey Reeves** likes to write books that help students figure out what they want to be when they grow up. She mostly lives in Washington, D.C., but spends as much time as she can in North Carolina and South Carolina with her grandkids.

# CONTENTS

# Finding an Animal-Friendly Career

Figuring out what you want to be when you grow up can be tricky. There are so many choices! How are you supposed to know which one to pick? Here's an idea... follow the clues!

The fact that you are reading a book called *Do You Like Taking Care of Animals?* is your first clue. It suggests that you have an interest in furry friends. True? If so, start looking at different careers where you can work with animals!

Your **interests** say a lot about who you are and what makes you tick. What do you like doing best?

**Abilities** are things that you are naturally good at doing. Another word for ability is talent. Everyone has natural talents and abilities. Some are more obvious than others. What are you really good at doing?

**Curiosity** offers up other career clues. To succeed in any career, you have to learn what it takes to do that job. You may have to go to college or trade school. It may take gaining new skills and getting experience. Curiosity about a subject keeps you at it until you learn what you need to know. What do you want to know more about?

Interests. Abilities. Curiosity. These clues can help you find a career that's right for you.

# FIND THE CLUES!

Each chapter includes several clues about careers you might enjoy.

INTERESTS: **What do you like doing?**

ABILITIES: **What are you good at doing?**

CURIOSITY: **What do you want to learn more about?**

# Are You a Future Animal Caregiver?

## WOULD YOU ENJOY...

**Working with animals to help people with health issues?** (see page 8)

**Teaching pets new tricks?** (see page 10)

**Protecting wildlife in a forest?** (see page 12)

**Working with crime-sniffing dogs?** (see page 14)

**Providing doggy day care services?** (see page 16)

**Exploring sea creatures in the ocean?** (see page 18)

**Giving pets new hairdos?** (see page 20)

**Taking care of other people's pets?** (see page 22)

**Helping sick animals get better?** (see page 24)

**Caring for animals in a zoo?** (see page 26)

## READ ON FOR MORE CLUES ABOUT CAREERS FOR KIDS WHO LOVE ANIMALS!

# Animal-assisted Therapist

**A person who connects people with pets to help treat mental and physical health conditions.**

A friendly dog and a wagging tail can make people smile. Animal-assisted therapists tap into this magic to help people feel better. They use highly-trained dogs to help treat people with all kinds of illnesses. They work in hospitals to support sick patients. They visit nursing homes to cheer up elderly people. They help people coping with **post-traumatic stress disorder** (PTSD). Therapists help patients feel safe and calmer with some fluffy canine cuddles.

# CLUES!

**INTEREST:** Helping people chill out

**ABILITY:** Sharing empathy and compassion with others

**CURIOSITY:** The healing powers of pets

# INVESTIGATE!

**NOW:** Try yoga, meditation, and other soothing activities.

**LATER:** Get training and certification in canine therapy.

# Animal Trainers

**A person who teaches animals how to behave.**

Sit! Stay! Come! Dogs that obey simple commands make life easier for the humans who love them. Dogs are smart. They can learn more than 100 human words. With patient coaching and plenty of practice, they learn how to behave and even perform tricks. Animal trainers sometimes train dogs to compete in shows. Some train service dogs to help people with **disabilities**. Trainers also work with horses, dolphins, and other animals. Trainers can be found anywhere you might find animals. They work in pet shops, kennels, zoos, aquariums, shelters, and private homes.

# CLUES!

**INTEREST:** Playing with pets

**ABILITY:** Teaching others how to do new things

**CURIOSITY:** How to motivate animals to learn

# INVESTIGATE!

**NOW:** Work on teaching a pet some new tricks.

**LATER:** Take animal training classes.

# Conservation Officer

**A person who protects wildlife and the environment.**

Conservation officers patrol the lands and waters of state and national parks. Another name for conservation officer is *game warden*. Protecting animals and nature is what they are all about. One way is to enforce laws about hunting and fishing. They educate people about wildlife and encourage them to take good care of natural resources. Sometimes they must capture animals that are causing problems. Other times they investigate damage to crops and property. In some cases, they help manage forest fires. A big perk of the job? Working outside in nature!

# CLUES!

**INTEREST:** Visiting state and national parks

**ABILITY:** Hunting, fishing, and other outdoor activities

**CURIOSITY:** Smart ways to conserve nature

# INVESTIGATE!

**NOW:** Take a hike in a forest.

**LATER:** Complete conservation officer training and a degree in conservation, wildlife management, or forestry.

# K-9 Officer

**A person who works with dogs to fight crime.**

Canine is another name for dog. K-9 police officers partner with highly trained dogs to fight crime. They train these dogs to do things like find drugs or bombs. In earthquakes and other disasters, K-9s help find and rescue people. The K-9's superpower is an amazing sense of smell. It can detect scents that a human nose cannot. Since they run fast, K-9s sometimes chase suspects. But fortunately for criminals, these dogs don't actually take a bite out of crime! Their human partners train them to respond instantly to commands and cues. K-9 dogs typically work for six to nine years.

# CLUES!

**INTEREST:** Fighting crime

**ABILITY:** Solving mysteries

**CURIOSITY:** How K-9 partners work together

# INVESTIGATE!

**NOW:** Ask a teacher or parent to help arrange a visit with your local K-9 police unit.

**LATER:** Earn a college degree in criminal justice.

# Kennel Manager

**A person who runs a pet boarding center.**

Doggy day care is a big deal these days. People board their pets when they work or go on vacation. It gives their pets a chance to play with furry "friends." Kennel managers run the places where pets come to stay. Lots of these places are more like pet spas. They have grooming services, playgrounds, and special snacks. Kennel managers train staff, take care of customers, and make sure the kennel is clean. These places are a home away from home for beloved pets. Keeping animals safe and happy is why kennel managers come to work every day.

# CLUES!

**INTEREST:** Taking care of stray animals

**ABILITY:** Hosting friends for fun visits

**CURIOSITY:** The business of pet care

# INVESTIGATE!

**NOW:** Visit different pet care centers to see what they are like.

**LATER:** Get experience working in a pet care center.

# Marine Biologist

**A person who studies life in the sea.**

**Marine** biologists work to learn all they can about life under the sea. Some work with familiar species like dolphins and whales. Others make new discoveries like the **apolemia**. This sea creature looks like someone threw a bunch of silly string in the ocean! Marine biologists look at how humans impact sea life. And they look at how sea life impacts humans. A big concern is all the plastics that get in waterways and harm sea creatures. If you were a marine biologist, how would you solve this problem?

# CLUES!

**INTEREST:** Sharks, dolphins, whales, and other things that live in the sea

**ABILITY:** Writing good research papers

**CURIOSITY:** Sea creatures still waiting to be discovered

# INVESTIGATE!

**NOW:** Visit a sea turtle hospital when you go to the beach.

**LATER:** Earn a college degree in marine biology.

# Pet Groomer

**A person who keeps pets looking good.**

Just like humans, pets need to be spruced up every once in a while. They need their fur cleaned and cut. They need their nails trimmed and their teeth brushed. People go to barber shops or hair salons to get this done. Pets go to a pet groomer. Pet groomers work with all kinds of breeds. A teddy bear cut looks cute on a **bichon**. That look would not work for a pit bull! Some pets are not happy about getting groomed. Pet groomers learn to handle the tough customers. Most of all, they enjoy keeping pets looking good!

# CLUES!

**INTEREST:** Taking care of animals

**ABILITY:** Treating friends to a new hairdo or manicure

**CURIOSITY:** The latest looks for furry friends

# INVESTIGATE!

**NOW:** Watch pet groomers in action at your local pet store.

**LATER:** Get training in pet grooming.

# Pet Sitter

**A person who cares for pets while their owners are away.**

When their families go away, some pets prefer to stay at their own home. Pet sitters provide these personal pet care services. Sometimes they go from one client's house to another. They walk and feed the pets and make sure all is okay. Other times, a pet sitter stays at the client's home. They take care of the pets and the house. Some pet sitters invite pets into their homes where they take care of several pets at once. Pet sitters run their own small businesses. They market their services on smartphone apps and with veterinarians.

# CLUES!

**INTEREST:** Spending time with pets

**ABILITY:** Babysitting neighbors' kids and pets

**CURIOSITY:** How to run your own pet business

# INVESTIGATE!

**NOW:** Volunteer to walk a neighbor's friendly dog.

**LATER:** Look into getting pet sitting training online.

# Vet Tech

**A person who helps care for animals in a clinic.**

Veterinarians, or vets, are doctors who care for animals. Vet techs are assistants who help veterinarians in animal clinics. In some ways, the work is like what nurses do to help medical doctors. Performing emergency first aid. Testing blood and other samples. Taking **x-rays**. Giving vaccine shots. Preparing animals for surgery. These are the jobs vet techs do every day! Their work is all about keeping animals healthy. Lots of vet techs work mostly with pets like cats and dogs. Some work with farm or zoo animals. The job outlook is good for animal lovers who care.

# CLUES!

**INTERESTS:** Coming to the rescue when someone gets hurt

**ABILITIES:** Staying calm under pressure

**CURIOSITY:** Health care for animals

# INVESTIGATE!

**NOW:** Find out what you can about pet first aid.

**LATER:** Earn a two-year college degree in veterinary care.

# Zookeeper

**A person who trains and cares for animals in a zoo.**

If you were a zookeeper, what types of animals would you most like to care for? The primates? Or the reptiles? Be extra careful if it's the big cats! There are so many great choices. Caring for most animals require the same types of tasks. There are cages to clean and poop to scoop. There is food to prepare. Each species requires a special diet. Elephants require about 350 pounds (159 kilograms) of vegetation each day. Lions prefer raw beef, chicken, sheep, and horse. Zookeepers also look for signs of injuries or illnesses. The more natural a **habitat** is, the more animals like it!

# CLUES!

**INTERESTS:** Visiting favorite animals at the zoo

**ABILITIES:** Taking responsibility for something other than yourself

**CURIOSITY:** Learning about different animal species

# INVESTIGATE!

**NOW:** Learn all you can about **endangered species.**

**LATER:** Earn a college degree in animal science, biology, or zoology.

# Wild Things Workshop

Keep investigating these career clues until you find a career that is right for you! Here are more ways to explore.

## Join a Club

Become a Junior Ranger with the National Park Service at: https://www.nps.gov/kids/become-a-junior-ranger.htm

## Talk to People with Interesting Careers

Ask your teacher or parent to help you connect with someone who has a career like the one you want. Be ready to ask lots of questions!

## Volunteer

Volunteer with your family at your local animal shelter.

## Enjoy Career Day

School career days can be a terrific way to find out more about different careers. Make the most of this opportunity.

## Explore Online

With adult supervision, use your favorite search engine to look online for information about careers you are interested in.

## Participate in Take Your Daughters and Sons to Work Day

Every year on the fourth Thursday of April, kids all over the world go to work with their parents or other trusted adults to find out what the world of work is really like.

Find out more at: https://daughtersandsonstowork.org

# Resources

### Animal Therapist
**YouTube: Why Does Pet Therapy Work?**
*https://www.youtube.com/watch?v=ODuRBPjoPrs*

### Animal Trainer
Moore, Arden. *A Kid's Guide to Dogs: How to Train, Care for, Play, and Communicate with Your Amazing Pet.* North Adams, MA: Storey Publishing, 2020.

### Conservation Officer
**National Park Foundation: Take a Virtual Visit to a National Park**
*https://www.nationalparks.org/connect/blog/take-virtual-visit-national-park*

### K-9 Officer
**YouTube: K-9 Patrol**
*https://www.youtube.com/watch?v=3OPOnVtKgTA*

### Kennel Manager
**American Kennel Club: Dog Breeds**
*https://www.akc.org/dog-breeds*

### Marine Biologist
**Nat Geographic Kids: Sea Life**
*https://www.natgeokids.com/ie/category/discover/
animals/sea-life*

### Pet Groomer
**PlayBarkRun: Dog Grooming Styles and Trims**
*https://www.playbarkrun.com/dog-grooming-styles-and-trims*

### Pet Sitter
Roberts, Willo Davis. *The Pet-Sitting Peril.* New York, NY:
Aladdin Books, 2016

### Vet Tech
**American Veterinary Medical Association:
First Aid Tips for Pet Owners**
*https://www.avma.org/resources/pet-owners/
emergencycare/first-aid-tips-pet-owners*

### Zookeeper
**YouTube: Be a Zookeeper**
*https://www.youtube.com/watch?v=jPwFXQQsFTY*

# Glossary

**abilities** (uh-BIH-luh-teez) natural talents or acquired skills

**apolemia** (AA-puh-leh-mee-uh) a type of stringy jellyfish-like creatures that live in the sea

**bichon** (BEE-shon) breed of small, sturdy dogs with thick, wavy white coats

**disabilities** (dih-suh-BIH-luh-teez) physical or mental conditions that limit a person's movements, senses, or activities

**curiosity** (kyur-ee-AH-suh-tee) strong desire to know or learn about something

**endangered species** (in-DAYN-juhrd SPEE-sheez) type of animal or plant that is at serious risk of dying out

**habitat** (HAH-buh-tat) natural home or environment of an animal or plant

**interests** (IN-tuh-ruhsts) things or activities that a person enjoys or is concerned about

**marine** (muh-REEN) of or relating to the sea or the plants and animals that live in the sea

**post-traumatic stress disorder** (pohst-truh-MAH-tik STREHS dis-OR-duhr) mental health disorder that some people develop after they experience or see a traumatic event

**x-rays** (EKS-rayz) imaging that creates pictures of the inside of the body

# Index